The Western Art of
Charles M. Russell

BALLANTINE BOOKS
A Division of Random House, Inc.
201 East 50th Street, New York, N.Y. 10022
Simultaneously published by
Ballantine Books, Ltd., Toronto, Canada

The Western Art of
Charles M. Russell

Edited by Lanning Aldrich

Ballantine Books, New York

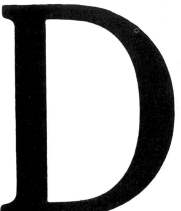**D**uring the forty-six years he called Montana home, Charlie Russell had hundreds of friends. They included substantial business people who helped his career, cowboys with whom he had ridden the range, and Indians with whom he had smoked the pipe. Everyone knew him as a great story-teller whose sense of the dramatic extended to a preference for eccentric dress, even in his later years. They remembered him as a night herder on the range, a bar companion, or a winter bunkmate who sold an occasional painting to keep food in the cupboard and drink on the table.

Though his friends came to realize that "Kid" Russell was a very good artist, it had never occurred to them to take his work seriously; after all, he did not himself. There came a time, however, when the rest of the world did take Russell's art seriously, and then his friends could not afford it. Many came to rue the day they lost or misplaced an illustrated card or letter—filled with misspelled humor and philosophy—gave away a painting, or allowed a piece of modeled clay or wax to melt in the sun.

There is remorse in Montana, too, because many great Russell paintings and sculptures—whole collections of them—found their way elsewhere, acquired by residents of other states who perceived their lasting greatness before Montanans did. It is considered a minor miracle, indeed, that two significant collections, those at the Russell Gallery in Great Falls and at the Montana Historical Society in Helena, are still there.

Although Charles M. Russell left nearly as great a legacy in the written word as he did on canvas and in clay and wax, he wrote very little about himself. He is an easily discernible figure in many of his paintings and in some of his published tales, but actual autobiographical material is almost nonexistent.

The exception is a spare little sketch he wrote in 1903 for a special edition of a Butte, Montana newspaper. "Mr. Russell was requested to prepare for the holiday *Inter Mountain* a sketch of his life, since no absolutely correct biography of this strange genius ever was published," said the editor in an opening statement. After "some persuasion," Russell sketched out his life, ending with the words, "Several papers have given me writeups, and though they were very kind and gave me much flattery, in many ways they were incorrect, so I have written you a few facts."

The facts were few, indeed. Charlie Russell was modest and, as with everything else about him, the modesty was genuine. He knew he was talented, but he had even that in perspective: "Talent, like a birth mark, is a gift and no credit nor fault to those who wear them." He would no doubt have been happiest with the kind of words that came to the Montana Historical Society just recently from a second-grade visitor: "I like evrythin' there and most I like that man who painted the pichers."

For all his modesty, Charles M. Russell was a unique and complex personality. While a "good mixer," he was essentially introspective and philosophical. He was humorous, yet melancholy, at times even faintly bitter. He was a working cowboy, yet not a skilled hand. He could not, or would not, spell anything right, but he was far from illiterate.

Charles Marion Russell was born in St. Louis, Missouri, on March 19, 1864, the son of extremely conservative parents who confidently expected that he would get an education and join the family's substantial coal and firebrick company. It was not to be. Charlie Russell hated school, its rules on behavior, as well as its lessons. He filled the margins of his textbooks with drawings; he daydreamed; he played hooky. Even a stint at military school did not have the desired effect. He began spending all his time on the waterfront, listening to the tales of the motley characters he met, mountain men, miners, riverboat sailors, cowboys. Most boys are infected only temporarily with the fever for adventure far from home, but with Charlie it was permanent. He wanted to go west, and he talked of nothing else.

Finally, in March, 1880, a week before his sixteenth birthday, the Russells gave their son permission to go to Montana. It was to be his birthday present, and they felt sure it would cure his wanderlust once and for all. There were, of course, some conditions: he was to accompany a family friend named Wallis "Pike" Miller, who had a part interest in a sheep ranch in the Judith Basin of Central Montana. Not only was Charlie to be under the protection of Pike Miller, his parents warned him, but he was to do as Pike told him. This last turned out to be a galling condition; nevertheless, it was through Pike Miller that Montana got her "Cowboy Artist." St. Louis would never again be home for Charlie Russell.

They traveled to the end of the new Utah Northern tracks, just across the Idaho—Montana border, and then by stagecoach to Helena. This roaring gold-camp, capital of the territory, was filled with the same kinds of frontier characters Russell had met on the waterfront back home. The wide-eyed boy from St. Louis took it all in. Pike and his young charge stayed in town just long enough to buy transport and supplies for the trip to the Miller ranch.

"I did not stay with Miller long as the sheep and I did not get along at all well," Russell wrote. "So we split up and I don't think Pike missed me much, as I was considered pretty ornery."

The Millers not only did not miss him much; they also apparently saw to it that a reputation as a "lazy, no good, ornery kid" followed him around. He applied for a job as a horse herder for the stage station at Utica, but was turned down.

This led to one of the most important chance events in Charlie's life. Dejected, Russell turned his horse away from the station and toward the Judith River. He made a lonely camp, where he was found by Jake Hoover, a man of vast frontier experience and remarkable sensitivity, who invited the youngster to share his food and campfire, then offered to take him to his cabin on the South Fork. Russell spent about two years with Hoover, and later frequently visited him when in the vicinity or down on his luck. Hoover had had so many experiences and was so willing to share them all that young Russell learned volumes from him.

In 1882 Charlie Russell returned to St. Louis, but he stayed only four weeks, in spite of pleas from his family. He bought some water colors and was soon on his way back to Montana, accompanied by his cousin, Jim Fulkerson. This lonesome youngster died of mountain fever in Billings, and Charlie, broke again and down on his luck, had to greet Jim's grieving family when they arrived to claim their son's body.

But it was not long before chance again favored him. When he pulled out of Billings with "200 miles between me and Hoover," he ran into a cow outfit with a thousand head of cattle ready to take on the trail to the Judith Basin roundup.

His reputation as a poor employment risk had apparently not reached these cattlemen, for he was hired to night-wrangle horses. "It was a lucky thing no one knew me or I'd never got the job," Russell recalled. Although cowhands who watched the herds at night were near the bottom of the range hierarchy, their responsibilities were serious enough; while Russell never claimed to be a top hand, he was able to say that "I held their bunch and at that time they had 300 saddle horses. That same fall old True hired me to night-herd his beef, and for 11 years I sung to their horses and cattle."

Many date Russell's fame to the terrible winter of 1886-1887, when alternate freezes and thaws destroyed thousands of head of cattle and wiped out many cow outfits. He was then working for the O-H brand, in central Montana, and his boss, Jesse Phelps, was trying also to keep his eye on a herd owned by Kaufman and Stadler of Helena. The owners had asked for an accounting by letter, and Phelps was trying to describe the fate of the cattle when Charlie Russell quickly painted a water color on a scrap of paper and told Phelps he could enclose it in the envelope. The small picture, called *Waiting for a Chinook* by its creator, but often known as *Last of Five Thousand,* shows a bony steer braced against the wind; two wolves wait for her to drop.

The sketch elicited so much attention in Helena and elsewhere that at least one man offered to pay for art lessons in Philadelphia for the promising young cowboy artist. But fate seems to have intervened, for Russell did not go to art school in Philadelphia, or anywhere else. Instead, he wandered up to Canada, where he spent six months with the Blood Indians. He was welcomed into their lodges and learned to speak in sign language. From then on, he favored the Indian point of view in all works; he portrayed whites as intruders, not as conquerors.

Although he was invited, Charlie Russell did not stay with the Indians. Instead, he rode south, and again fell in with the right people at the right time. Almost broke and wearing worn-out clothes that he had augmented with a few Indian items, he met a long train of overland freight wagons bound south with a load of furs. Not only did this bring him the freighting experience that is reflected in many of his greatest paintings, it also assured him grub and shelter. He left the train before it reached the head of Missouri River navigation at Fort Benton, and headed once more for the warmth of Jake Hoover's cabin.

"In the spring of 1889, I went back to the Judith, taking my old place wrangling," Russell wrote. "The Judith country was getting pretty well settled and sheep had the range, so the cow men decided to move. All that summer and the next we trailed the cattle north to Milk river. In the fall of 1891, I received a letter from Charles Green, better known as 'Pretty Charlie,' a bartender who was in Great Falls, saying that if I could come to that camp I could make $75 a month

and grub. It looked good, so I saddled my gray and packed Monty, my pinto, and pulled my freight for said berg.

"When I arrived I was introduced to Mr. G., who pulled a contract as long as a stake rope for me to sign. Everything I drew, modeled or painted was to be his, and it was for a year. I balked. Then he wanted me to paint from six in the morning till six at night, but I argued that there was some difference in painting and sawing wood, so we split up and I went to work for myself."

This was the final, significant turning point in his artistic life; although he spent several more years in the old, drifting style, Charlie Russell had become a serious painter. As he reported it, "The feed was very short at times, but we wintered. Next spring I went back to Milk river and once more took to the range. In the fall I returned to Great Falls, took up the paint brush and have never 'sung to them' since."

Charlie Russell realized that what happened to him in 1896 was the most providential event of all. "I went to Cascade in the fall of '95 and was married to Nancy Cooper in '96. She took me for better or worse, and I will leave it to her which she got. We moved to Great Falls in '97 and have lived there ever since."

Nancy Cooper was sixteen years old when Charlie met her, and he was thirty-one. It was the general opinion around Montana that Nancy was too hard on Charlie, keeping him at his easel and away from his old friends and entertainments, but Russell himself never complained. Although there were several years of financial struggle, the stubborn little business manager, firmly convinced of her husband's genius, eventually won success and national recognition for him.

As the years passed, Charlie Russell settled down. When ill health first began plaguing him, a note of sadness crept into his work, and also into letters to his friends. In 1925, he went to the Mayo Clinic in Rochester, Minnesota. The reluctant doctors found it necessary to inform Russell that he did not have long to live. He and Nancy returned to Great Falls, and on Sunday, October 14, 1926, he died of a heart attack. He was sixty-two years old. His funeral, its procession unmechanized at Russell's request, was attended by hundreds of people who, in their age and station, reflected Charlie Russell's magnetism: little children, old cowboy buddies, and many Indians. Among the honorary pallbearers were his good friends Will Rogers, Irvin S. Cobb, and William S. Hart.

It now is clear that Charles Marion Russell himself did not realize how great a legacy he was to leave. Its richness is indisputable: he came to Montana just in time to see the passing of the frontier, and he had the talent and the instinct to record it. He came not to paint or sketch or model, but to live; he wanted to be a cowboy, not a famous artist. That he became both, and at precisely the right time, resulted in a body of art and literature whose universal value is impossible to overstate.

VIVIAN A. PALADIN, Editor
Montana The Magazine of Western History
The Montana Historical Society
Helena, Montana
May, 1975

(5)
INDIAN WOMEN MOVING (On The Move) • 1898
24¼ x 36, oil
Courtesy Amon Carter Museum, Fort Worth, Texas

(6)
A DESPERATE STAND • 1898
24⅛x36⅛, oil
Courtesy Amon Carter Museum, Fort Worth, Texas

(8)
WAGON BOSS • 1909
36x23½, oil
Courtesy Thomas Gilcrease Institute of American History and Art, Tulsa, Oklahoma

(9)
A TIGHT DALLY AND A LOOSE LATIGO • 1920
$30\frac{1}{8}$x$40\frac{1}{2}$, oil
Courtesy Amon Carter Museum, Fort Worth, Texas

(10)
LEWIS AND CLARK MEETING INDIANS AT ROSS' HOLE • 1912
11'5¼ x24'9, oil
Courtesy Montana Historical Society, Helena, Montana

(12)
YORK · 1908
19x25½ , watercolor
Courtesy Montana Historical Society, Helena, Montana

(14)
STOLEN HORSES • 1898
18x24 , oil
Courtesy Rockwell-Corning Museum, Corning, New York

(15)
JERKED DOWN • 1907
36x22, oil
Courtesy Thomas Gilcrease Institute of American History and Art, Tulsa, Oklahoma

(16)
THE MEDICINE MAN • 1908
29¾ x48, oil
Courtesy Amon Carter Museum, Fort Worth, Texas

(19)
KEEOMA No. 3 • 1898
18¼ x 24¼ , oil
Courtesy Montana Historical Society, Helena, Montana

(20)
THE ROUNDUP • 1913
25x49, oil
Mackay Collection
Courtesy Montana Historical Society, Helena, Montana

(22)
THE HERD QUITTER • 1897
20x30½ , oil
Courtesy Montana Historical Society, Helena, Montana

(23)
FOLLOWING THE BUFFALO RUN • 1894
23⅛x35, oil
Courtesy Amon Carter Museum, Fort Worth, Texas

(24)
WHEN HORSE FLESH COMES HIGH · 1909
24¼ x 36¼ , oil
Courtesy Amon Carter Museum, Fort Worth, Texas

(25)
FREE TRAPPERS · 1911
33x23¾ , oil
Mackay Collection
Courtesy Montana Historical Society, Helena, Montana

(26)
THE ATTACK • 1900
18½x24⅜, oil
Courtesy Amon Carter Museum, Fort Worth, Texas

(29)
WHEN SIOUX AND BLACKFEET MEET · 1903
27¼ x 16½ , watercolor
Courtesy Thomas Gilcrease Institute of American History and Art, Tulsa, Oklahoma

(30)
THE BROKEN ROPE • 1904
24x36⅛, oil
Courtesy Amon Carter Museum, Fort Worth, Texas

(31)
FIREBOAT • 1918
15¼ x 24½ , oil
Courtesy C. M. Russell Museum, Great Falls, Montana

(33)
WHEN HORSES TALK WAR THERE'S
SMALL CHANCE FOR PEACE   •   1915
24¼ x 36½ , oil
Mackay Collection
Courtesy Montana Historical Society, Helena, Montana

(35)
SMOKE OF A .45 • 1908
24 ¼ x 36, oil
Courtesy Amon Carter Museum, Fort Worth, Texas

(36)
BRINGING HOME THE MEAT · 1891
36⅛ x 24, oil
Courtesy Amon Carter Museum, Fort Worth, Texas

(38)
BRONC IN COW CAMP · 1897
20⅛x31¼ , oil
Courtesy Amon Carter Museum, Fort Worth, Texas

(39)
MEN OF THE OPEN RANGE • 1923
24x36, oil
Mackay Collection
Courtesy Montana Historical Society, Helena, Montana

(41)
WILD HORSE HUNTERS • 1913
30x47, oil
Courtesy Amon Carter Museum, Fort Worth, Texas

(43)
WHEN COWS WERE WILD · 1926
19½ x 29, watercolor
Courtesy Montana Historical Society, Helena, Montana

(44)
BESTED • 1895
23 x 35, oil
Courtesy Amon Carter Museum, Fort Worth, Texas